Science STARTS

A+ books

BUBBLES FLOAT, BUBBLES POP

by Mark Weakland

School District 64
164 S. Prospect
Park Ridge, IL 60068

CAPSTONE PRESS
a capstone imprint

With a puff of air, bubbles appear like magic.
Shimmering, they float through the sunlight.
Do you know how bubbles are made?

3

Every bubble is a round pocket of gas.

4

Like balloons, bubbles trap gas within a thin skin.

Bubbles form in cold or hot liquids. In a cold glass of soda, bubbles stick to a cherry.

In boiling water, bubbles sparkle like diamonds.

POP!

8

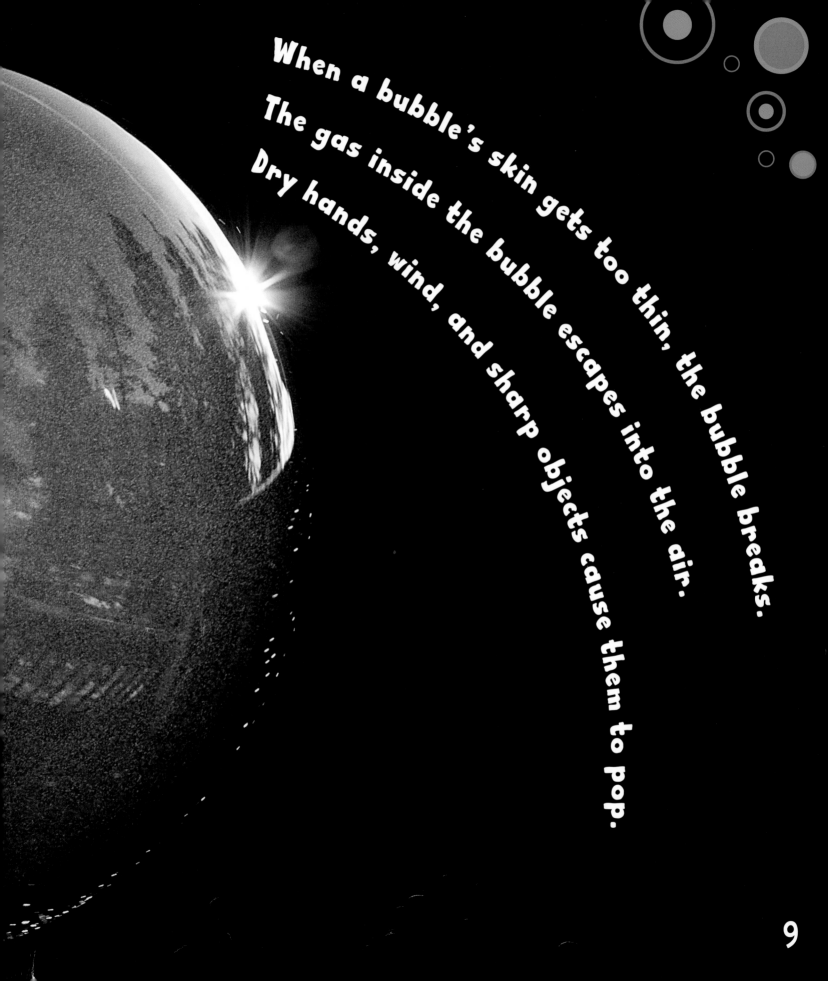

When a bubble's skin gets too thin, the bubble breaks. The gas inside the bubble escapes into the air. Dry hands, wind, and sharp objects cause them to pop.

9

Bubbles always form in the same shape—a sphere. A sphere is perfectly round.

Why are bubbles spheres? Why aren't they ovals or cubes? A sphere is a strong shape. For its size, a sphere can hold a large amount of gas.

You can make bubbles by blowing air into a liquid, but these bubbles quickly pop.

You might see air bubbles in a fish tank. Air bubbles add oxygen to the water.

13

Soap lets you blow bubbles that are less likely to break. Because their soapy skin stretches, soap bubbles last longer than air bubbles.

Can you touch a soap bubble? To hold a soap bubble, wet your hands with soap solution. Then gently catch a bubble with your hands.

Have you blown a bubble with soft, gooey bubble gum? As you blow in air, the gum stretches and the bubble grows.

18

The world's largest bubble gum bubble was almost 2 feet (.6 meter) across! What will happen when the gum gets stretched too thin?

George Washington School
Learning Resource Center

19

Nature is full of bubbles. They sparkle in streams.

They froth and foam at the beach. Look for bubbles wherever there is water.

Some gas bubbles grow deep in the earth.
They push through pools of mud.

Finally, mud bubbles burst with a squishy plop. Yuck! Now the air stinks.

23

A spittlebug surrounds itself with bubbles. Hiding in bubbly foam, a young spittlebug is protected from its enemies.

A polar bear swims under water. As it swims, it exhales or breathes out bubbles of air.

In a tub or pool, you can blow bubbles too. Just breathe out under water.

Every bubble is a tiny world. Look closely.

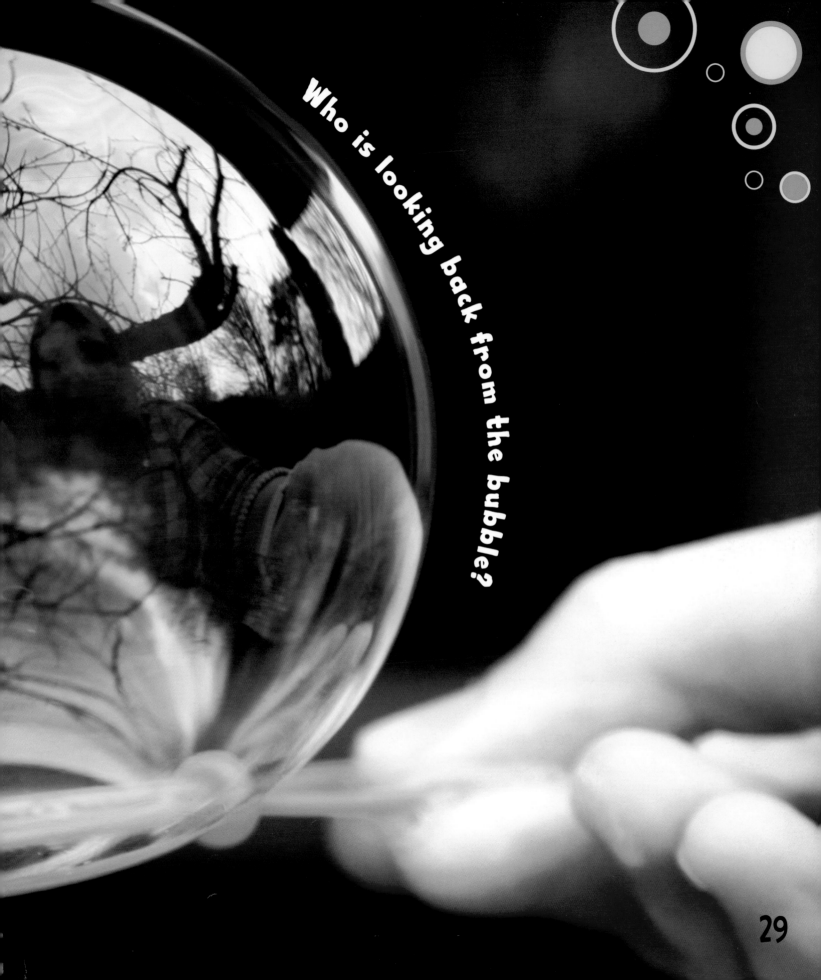

Who is looking back from the bubble?

Glossary

foam—a thick mixture of many small bubbles

froth—many small bubbles

gas—a substance that spreads to fill any space that holds it

shimmer—to shine or sparkle

sphere—a perfectly round shape like a ball or globe

Read MORE

Bayrock, Fiona. *Bubble Homes and Fish Farts.* Watertown, Mass.: Charlesbridge, 2009.

McCarthy, Meghan. *Pop!: The Accidental Invention of Bubble Gum.* New York: Simon & Schuster Books for Young Readers, 2010.

Shores, Erika. *How to Make Bubbles.* Hands-On Science Fun. Mankato, Minn.: Capstone Press, 2011.

Internet SITES

FactHound offers a safe, fun way to find Internet sites related to this book. All of the sites on FactHound have been researched by our staff.

Here's all you do:

Visit *www.facthound.com*

Type in this code: 9781429652506

Super-cool stuff!

Check out projects, games and lots more at **www.capstonekids.com**

Index

air, 3, 9, 13, 14, 18, 23
balloons, 5
beaches, 21
boiling, 7
breathing, 26, 27
bubble gum, 18, 19

gas, 4, 5, 9, 11, 22
liquids, 6, 13
mud, 22, 23
popping, 9, 13
skin, 5, 9, 14

soap, 14, 16
soda, 6
spheres, 10, 11
spittlebugs, 25
streams, 20

A+ Books are published by
Capstone Press,
151 Good Counsel Drive, P.O. Box 669,
Mankato, Minnesota 56002.
www.capstonepub.com

Books published by Capstone Press are manufactured with paper
containing at least 10 percent post-consumer waste.

Library of Congress Cataloging-in-Publication Data
Weakland, Mark.
    Bubbles float, bubbles pop / by Mark Weakland.
        p. cm.—(A+ books. Science starts)
    Includes bibliographical references and index.
        Summary: "Simple text and photographs explain the basic science behind bubbles"—Provided by publisher.
            ISBN 978-1-4296-5250-6 (library binding)
            ISBN 978-1-4296-6141-6 (paperback)
                1. Bubbles—Juvenile literature. I. Title.
                QC183.S25 2011
                530.4'275—dc22   2010038874

Credits

Jenny Marks, editor; Alison Thiele, designer; Marcie Spence, media researcher; Eric Manske, production specialist

Photo Credits

Capstone Studio: Karon Dubke, cover; Dr. Peter Schmidt, 26–27; Getty Images Inc.: Jodie Wallis/Flickr, 28–29; iStockphoto: AlasdairJames, 24–25, AlexeyStoyanov, 20, RyanLane, 18–19, Yildizbasoglu, 12–13; Shutterstock: Brisbane, 16–17, Dmitriy Shironosov, 1, Hallgerd, 4–5, happytan, 2–3, kenee (design element), MaleWitch, 14–15, M_A_R_G_O (design element), photostudio7 (design element), Quayside, 6, Robyn Mackenzie, 21, Roman Sigaev, 7, Steffen Foerster Photography, 22–23, Suzi Nelson, 10–11; Tom Falconer, 8–9.

Note to Parents, Teachers, and Librarians

The Science Stars series supports national education standards related to science. This book describes and illustrates bubbles. The images support early readers in understanding the text. The repetition of words and phrases helps early readers learn new words. This book also introduces early readers to subject-specific vocabulary words, which are defined in the Glossary section. Early readers may need assistance to read some words and to use the Table of Contents, Glossary, Read More, Internet Sites, and Index sections of the book.

Printed in the United States of America in North Mankato, Minnesota.
092010   005933CGS11

School District 64
164 S. Prospect
Park Ridge, IL 60068